A CONVERSATION...., A CONTACT

A collection of flash-fictions, auto-fictions, hybrid tales, letters, dream casting, dramatic sketches, semi-short fictions, prosaic experiments, chain-fictions...

Tendai Rinos Mwanaka

Mwanaka Media and Publishing Pvt Ltd,
Chitungwiza Zimbabwe

*

Creativity, Wisdom and Beauty

Publisher:

Mmap

Mwanaka Media and Publishing Pvt Ltd

24 Svosve Road, Zengeza 1

Chitungwiza Zimbabwe

mwanaka@yahoo.com

https//mwanakamediaandpublishing.weebly.com

Distributed in and outside N. America by African Books Collective

orders@africanbookscollective.com

www.africanbookscollective.com

ISBN: 978-0-7974-9440-4

EAN: 9780797494404

© Tendai Rinos Mwanaka 2018

DISCLAIMER

All views expressed in this publication are those of the author and do not
necessarily reflect the views of *Mmap*.

Table of Contents

Part 1: A Contact

A Conversation....., A Contact:..2

Finding Trouble:..3

Staying With Grandma Helen:..4

Raising A Cain Again:..6

Mandela's Dreams:...7

You Also Must Run..., Faster:...8

Part 2: ......,

Dear Mom:...10

Rihhana And Chris:...13

One Day So Longer Ago:..17

She Is Now A Prostitute:..19

Especially For T:...22

When He Was Far From Home:.......................................25

The Girl Right Across The Street:....................................27

Plan B:...30

The Eagle Prophetess:...33

Part 3: A Conversation

The Promises Of Love:...35

Your love mirror

Love

The language of love

The eye of the bull

Patricia

Pain-sites

- Grandmother
- Portraits in the darkness
- The language of the truth
- Shadows
- Misheck
- Drinking himself to death
- Keche's death
- Suicide
- At the grave place
  Leonard:……………………………………………………..53
  Running/Snakes/Tsunamis/Mountains…:………………..................58
- Snakes, Snakes, Snakes…
- Tsunamis, Tsunamis, Tsunamis…
- The Wolf Cousin
- At Internet Cafe
- Don't Dream, don't dream, don't dream…
- Running, Running, Running…
- The Lion
- Up The Mountains
  WhatsApp Love:…………………………………………...69
  Their marriage:………………………………………...................74
- She had to talk to him
- Be-Longing
- Parallel Environments
- Blindfold Identity
- Their Wedding
- Their Marriage.., a train
- Their Lovemaking.., their infidelity
- Foreplay

Her other mouth
His thrusts..., her trusting...
After reading Arja Salafranca's poem, "Snake"
Her Struggles
Calling herself away
What she had talked about
Their life together
What she couldn't understand
Ploughing/Accident/Hurricane...:....................................91
Karidza:.. 94

Introduction

Some many years ago, around the turn of the century, I wrote stories around the collection, *An Unfinished Circle*, most of which have been published in my previous 2 books of short stories, *Keys in the River*, and *Finding a Way Home*, but few short fictions, what one reviewer back then called *small vignettes* couldn't make the above collections. That reviewer, reviewing for a South African fiction publisher felt these small pieces wouldn't hold in the book, felt they were suitable for magazine publication. Back then the flash fiction genre wasn't well known in Africa, so I suppose to this reviewer there was no sense in publishing these small pieces in book form. Later, I begun to know about this genre of fictions and realised I was already writing these before I knew what they were. Nearly twenty years later I have collected some of these short fictions and many others I wrote along the way to make this collection, *A Conversation…, A Contact*

And it's exactly one of these earlier pieces that rent out to this collection its title, *A Conversation…, A Contact*, which is just two lines long but contains the whole collection into its many meaning worlds. This sketchy dramatic piece is a conversation between two very interesting animals, Frog and Caterpillar. I have written about the frog before, in a story *And These Were Their Reasons*, in *Finding a Way Home*. Growing up in the rural areas, these two animals were connected together by water, as in water in the river for a frog, and water as rain for the caterpillar.

But they were not well liked animals in my universe. I don't remember any child or adult who touch and played with a frog;

neither could we eat it as in some cultures like the French. Frogs have this ability to jump around every few minutes. It's difficult to catch it around the river. Frogs were thought to have poison, the caterpillars insides were dangerous to teeth, would decay them. Yet we enjoyed teasing the caterpillar whilst dragging its feet after a rainy day, it would ball into a ring and wouldn't release itself until you stop teasing it, caterpillars have an undying spirit too, if it gets cut by the middle, the head part will continue moving. I am not sure whether it would heal eventually, but it won't stop moving.

The frog has a great ingratiating quality too, its music making ability. You would know when the frogs start baying in the river it was time to go home, it was night. I remember those early evenings we would refuse letting go fishing as the sun goes down, you listen to the frogs, and fish is so responsive to your bait, you know you need those few hours of early dusk to catch enough food for the night for a big family of 10 people, and these frogs provided accompanying music. It's pleasurable to just watch a caterpillar's legs synchronically jellying as they move, no leg moves out of tune with the rest. But in this collection they start my story, each mocking the other for their uncanny abilities, the frog tells the caterpillar to *stop dragging its feet*, the caterpillar tells the frog to *stop jumping into conclusions*.

This collection is arranged into 3 parts, and each part has an insight into the meaning worlds of the collection's title. The first part is entitled, *A Contact*. A Contact begins everything between any two entities or more. In this section I am trying, as a story teller to create that first contact between me and my readers. The six pieces in this section are, *A Conversation....., A Contact, Finding Trouble, Staying With Grandma Helen, Raising A Cain Again, Mandela's Dreams, You Also Must Run..., Faster.*

Each is a contact into the areas I will be tackling throughout the collection. The first one, *A Conversation...., A Contact*, I warn my readers not to rush into conclusion, but also when I experiment, which is at the heart of the whole collection and my work, generally; not to drag their feet. The second one, *Finding Trouble,* is on love, the difficulty in trying to find love, the long journey one might travel to get there, and when they arrive all that they find is trouble, so this story is a contact into the love and relationship stories upcoming. The third one, *Staying With Grandma Helen* represent the storyteller, represent me the writer, represent the strange stories I grew up hearing from Grandmother Helen. It is the source of my art. The fourth one, *Raising A Cain Again,* represent stories on political strife my country went through, how it can be linked to the bible story of Cain and Abel, where we saw a brother killing his own brother, *Mandela dreams* represent the dream stories in the collection. Dreams are at the heart of my talent too. Mandela created dreams that touched every human being he got in touch with. So for me dreams whether sleeping dreams or wide awake dreams, represent a person's humanity and can light worlds for others. And the last story in this section, *You Also Must Run..., Faster* is another warning. Why is the character running, there is a storm. And it's a bird that tells him to run, the Rain bird. The act of running or moving, I have come to realise, is at the heart of who I am too. I am always running, moving in my dreams, even waking dreams. I always want to see myself moving onto another perspective. And a line in this piece becomes the heart of this section.

Pieces in this section are small flash fiction pieces. Each ends before you even start, but it stays in. A good flash fiction piece, or writer just doesn't show you the story; they go further by transporting the reader into the mysterious, strange, or creepy worlds of the story. It's up to the reader to enter into these worlds of the story and define meaning. Flash fictions, like the flash of a camera, are sudden, brief, photographic writing that gives flash glints into the larger story. Usually it doesn't follow a narrative linear of storytelling.

But if you had rushed into conclusion that this is a collection of flash fictions, not only are you going to be confounded in the next section, which is part of the title of the collection's title, the ...., part of it. For me this part refuses to settle. Its starts the experimentation, it ambles wherever with the reader. There are letters as in the pieces, *Dear Momma*, and *Especially For T*, and there are longer flash fiction pieces in *Plan B*. There is the grandma tales in strangeness and hybridization in *One Day So Longer Ago*, and *Eagle Prophetess*, and there are love and relationships stories in *Especially For T, The Girl Right Across The Street, She Is Now A Prostitute*, and *Rihhana And Chris*. There are auto fictions as in *When He Was So Far From Home,* and there is the trying to understand what home entails in the previous story and in *Dear Momma*

Part 3 represent the last part of the title, which is *Conversation*. In this part we have longer fictions, the conversations deepen. We have dream scopes, we have chain fictions, and we have the mixing of poetry and fiction to create what I might term experimental prosaic pieces.

A Conversation..., A Contact has 22 fiction pieces around themes to do with political struggle, love relationships, heartbreaks and the resulting breakdowns, dreams, folklores, life, spirituality, anger, hate, grief, and all sorts of other human breaths. It acts as that light touch that torches our endeavours and make us come to terms with the world around and inside us through the act of creating bridges. Its art is in creating brief human encounters and touches that grow into mysteries, some strange, some miraculous, some fulfilling.

PART 1: A CONTACT

In which,

I looked at Muchena Mountains … and then, I started running.

A Conversation...., A Contact.

**C**aterpillar: "Don't jump into conclusions."
Frog: "Don't drag your feet."

Finding Trouble

She says I should call her if ever I find trouble, so I start looking for Trouble in the Student Companion book and when I fail to find it by the end of my seventh grade: I start looking for it in the Dictionary through my secondary and high school years, until I got to the Taisekwas, Tarisais, Tinotendas...

Way later in life, still looking for Trouble, I found it in the Encyclopedia, in the middle of the Ts. So, I called her to tell her I had found her.

Staying With Grandma Helen

There were the days he was staying with his Grandma Helen, in his late primary school days. His Mom was just some few metres away from Grandma's hut, with the rest of the family. His mother said she missed him. She felt he was a child she had given birth to but denied herself full motherhood. It's never easy to allow another woman to raise your child, even for a good cause. It's always a big sacrifice. He also wished, sometimes, that he was staying with Mom, yet he wanted to be with Grandma. It was easier when his Mom was not around, was in Harare with his father. It meant his brother would be with him, staying with Grandma, too. The two would encourage each other, and go out together to fetch the firewood, in the dark summer nights. Grandma Helen would be telling them ghost or zombie stories and they would be afraid to get outside to fetch the firewood. The zombies and ghosts were outside, waiting for them like the dry thirsty land that waits for the first rains of a new year.

When he was staying alone with Grandma, he would refuse to go outside. Inversely, he would hear fewer stories because they would go to sleep earlier, once they finish eating. Staying with Grandma when Mom was there had its benefits. He would know when he arrives home from school he would have double of food things waiting for him. He would first go to his Mom's place and eat whatever she had left for him. She always left out something of her longing soul for him, despite the fact that he was staying with Grandma, and then he would go back to Grandma's place and eat what she had prepared for him. It was even advantageous because Grandma always cooked traditional foods that were rare and the treat was always delicious. You might term him a foodie if you are into that sort of thing- of naming things, people...

All the other siblings envied him, and had jostled with him for his position. He wouldn't let go this heaven. He thinks Grandma also enjoyed staying with him. He was grandma's special man. He was the grandfather he never saw. Grandma always said she doesn't need any other Grandchildren, but him.

As the protagonist of his Grandma's heart, his Mom's soul, his siblings' intense envy and rivalry, he enjoyed these stories he would hear from the awesome storytellers- his family were- more especially from his Mom and Grandma.

Raising A Cain Again

They were brothers from the same womb, Cain and Abel. Cain brought to the Lord produce from his fields, which was not good enough in the eyes of the Lord. Abel brought fat portions from some of the firstborns of his flock, which pleased the Lord.

Cain killed Abel.

I know I am not saying anything new here. You have already heard of this story,

77 times!

And then the Lord asked Cain, "Where is your brother, Abel."

And he replied,

"I don't know, am I my brother's killer?"

Mandela's Dreams

On a breezy sunny day we drove up to the north side of Johannesburg with my cousins, Bernard and Wycliffe. We saw beautiful buildings, green-parks, flowers, artefacts and Mandela's metal sculpture loomed large as you enter Sandton.

He is overrated, says Wycliffe.

I love the written word, so I hear Mandela whispering in my ears ...*As you let your light shine you unconsciously give others the permission to do the same.*

Nope.., a Messiah fool, says Bernard.

******

We came through Houghton Park on our way back to the east where we stayed, we hoped for a glimpse of him, but could only content with his dreams.

The future belongs to those who believe in the beauty of their dreams.

You Also Must Run.... faster

And then I heard the sound of the bird crying. I thought I hadn't heard well, so I listened intently again, and then I heard it again. It was the forlorn warning cry of the Rain bird.

It said.

"Haya-aa! Haya-aa! Haya-aaa! Tsvotsvotsvoo! Tsvotsvotsvoo! Tsvotsvotsvoo! Haya-aa! Haya-aa! Haya-aaa…"

It was unmistakable.

"The storm is coming"

It also meant.

"You also must run…. Faster."

I looked at Muchena Mountains … and then, I started running.

PART 2: ......,

And

Everything was crazy, good crazy, nutty crazy…

Dear Momma

You are 65 years old this day, 23 August 2014, and yet 30 years ago you were a beautiful rose. Now you are an old evergreen Munhacha tree (Parinari curatellifolio), so abundant with sweet fruits. Everything was crazy, good crazy, nutty crazy, you used to captivate us with your laughing mind, a mind full of life, humour, mischief, especially when we came off age and became boys-to-men or men, and girls-to-women or women. It is a mind that made us realise we can laugh at anything in life, that we shouldn't always take ourselves seriously, but what we do.

In those distant mountains of childhood, you were the girl we started looking for in every girl we met, we loved, we adored, we crushed over, but none stayed long in us to take your space in us. I love you momma, even now as I realise finding you in another girl is just a pipe dream because I can't recreate you in them.

I know you are out there, over 300kms away from where I am, and it's unfortunate that we don't talk as often as I would have loved, but I love you. You are all in me, somewhere inside me, every minute of me. I am sorry life has happened between us this way. I know you feel I have abandoned you as you deal with the softening light in you. In this soft dim light of your kitchen, a thatched hut brimming with cooking smokes and smells, I wonder, with watered mouth, what delicious foods you still create in those black clay pots. The black clay pots you fashioned out with your own bare hands!

Grace, you were mother-hen over your brood, you were our reliable doctor, and doctoring everything away from us with shrubs, roots, bucks, stems, soil, water, ash…you cured every ill, every cough, every whine, everything. You were our older brother, our sisters' older sister; you protected us against bullies, conniving girls and boys, hurtful neighbours and strangers, against our own softness and hotness.

You were our Granny; you told us stories, tales, metaphors, proverbs, pushed our minds, seeded this speckle of fire in this pen. You told stories to cut reality down to size for us, so we could confront it and give ourselves some sense of control. You were our friend, never refusing us our right to be who we wanted to be; you would take the back seat when we wanted to strike out on our own- a compass arrow, seeing things- even when you knew it was a hard direction, or that we might never reach our destination.

You cried with us when life offered us vinegar and pepper instead of sugar. Do you remember that day in 1993 when I got my 'O' level English result slip, with a grade D fail. I had cried all the way home, but when you saw me you started crying too. You knew I had failed it even before I could tell you. We hugged and cried together, and then I left you back for school. Now, I know you sometimes cry when you think of all these memories, all the love, all the hopes you had for us, all the hopes we had for ourselves, and I hope they have all become finer and beautiful, grounded to smoothness by the years.

You were our greatest teacher. You taught us to be straight talking, upfront, honest, tough but fair. To call a spade a spade, you taught us how to cut through society, culture and life's bull crap, and get to the crux of the matter. You taught us the answers weren't out there, but inside us waiting to be discovered. You taught us to realise

11

that life doesn't owe us anything, that we can take what we want, and leave what we do not want, and that, it's what we make out of this life that we deserve, or that would mean something worthwhile to us.

Grace, you were our home, you are still my home. You are home as spiritual truth, longing and grace.

Rihhana And Chris

he
is black,
with a white spot
under her neck. He has dark
black-greyish stripes. The two have been
all over our places. Sometimes she gets in my house
I don't even know why I have prefixed her a she and him
a he. She could be him or he could be her. Him or her, maybe
it's the way the two behave that makes me think she is Rihhana
and he is Chris. I call her Rihhana, anyway. She is not similar
to that daughter of yours you call Rihhana. Your daughter
doesn't even have the rihhanarish looks; a big forehead,
petite lips and the knack for naughtiness. I have
tried to be unthreatening to her, all the
last six months, to encourage
her to have a little
trust for me,
in me,
but
it's
getting
such that I am
worried she would

never trust me. She is
defiantly staying away from
my reach, and I can't get closer. She
would run off if I did. But, I am not giving up
on her. Sometimes she stares at me; eyes feral, icy,
inscrutable, and I stare back at Riri. Some pair of irises
that looks like overlapping parenthesis, or with a
dollar sign in them- is that what she is seeing,
I don't know! But, I stare back intently at
Riri. I am defiant in my want to
have a relationship
with her. She
is the alley
cat
that strays
at my property,
usually on top of the
roof. Sometimes, in the cold
months, she spends the nights
whinnying, mewing, and painful like a
small tot, from the cold biting into her woolies
blanket, especially in nights when the mercury
hits the negatives. I wish I could help. I
understand that pain; it's a deep
gutted pain. I have tried to
encourage Rihhana to
make friends with
me. She is the
first alley

14

cat
I have
tried to have
a relationship with,
and even allowed to enter
my house. I have never encouraged
Chris, but nowadays I barely acknowledge
him because he is with Rihhana, on and offish. I
think he strays somewhere else, nowadays. But
sometimes he comes home, especially
at night. Nobody likes Chris in the
surrounding area. People
around the place
wanted him
away,
so
they
would throw
stones at him. I think,
eventually he had had enough of all
this unearned angst against him, and left
It's his eyes that aren't right- there is always
something sitting there, talking to you,
something with no human character
It stripes you naked and people
don't want to feel naked,
at that, on the outside,
during day
hours,

so
they
always stoned
him off their sights
Only for Chris to return at
night, once in a while, and
Rihhana and Chris would growl,
fight, and create noise on top of
the roof and we wouldn't sleep
those nights. I suppose Chris is
still attracted to Rihhana,
that's why he comes,
once in a while,
and they
would
make
love
I
hope
Rihhana is
putting on protection
Chris has never really been
interested in condoms. I don't
want to have to deal with a
litter of babies, especially
babies with the
rowdy blood
of Chris
No!

One Day So Longer Ago

"**O**nce upon a time..," my grandma would start the story, "one day not so long ago, it happened that there was a certain family that lived a solitary existence." She would tell me that there was a death in this family. The old lady of this family died but the rest of the family didn't know that she was dead. This young family hadn't known about people dying because it had never occurred to them in their living memories. So, they kept the corpse of their Granny with them.

In the kitchen they would help it into a sitting position by leaning it against the walls. They also made conversation with it. What baffled them was that their Granny seemed no longer disposed to talking, yet to their greater confusion, she still could smile and stare endlessly. What also troubled them was why she had given up on most of the things she used to do, as if she had lost the will to live. The mother of all that baffled them was why she had started producing a smelly ardour, which was now being felt all over the household. Every night they would take their Granny with them to their sleeping quarters. It was on the fifth day when a certain old man from a far of place passed by their homesteads. He was left aghast and at the edge of sense by the smell of the decomposing corpse and the innocent ignorance of this household.

He had to perform to the best of his ability in order to convince them that their Grandmother was dead and decaying. He also told them that the smelly ardour was coming from her decaying body. She had to be buried in order to rid themselves of that ardour. So, altogether with that old man, they dug her grave and buried her.

This household was convinced beyond doubt when a couple of days, after the burial of their Granny, that smelly ardour was no longer felt anywhere around the homesteads. Then, it happened that another day, not so long after this occurrence, they were sited after a bountiful meal of boiled eggs, beans and Sadza when one of their children puffed. The smell was so over-powering that they were convinced and could even concur with this child that he was dead. So they buried this young child alive. It happened again with another of their children and, they buried this child alive. When all their children and the father of this household had all been buried alive, and the wife was in the process of digging her own grave to bury herself alive after finding that at one time she had smelled badly, that old man who had passed by this homestead, a few months before, came through on his way back.

He searched around the homesteads for people but couldn't find any, and in a very high voice, he called.

"Where are you, people of this homestead?"

The wife, amid her labouring, heard this old man, and called back.

"We are all here, we are all dead."

Upon which the old man went to the graveyard which was just outside the homesteads.

Surely the whole household had died, except for this woman who was meanwhile trying to bury herself alive.

She Is Now A Prostitute

She was a sweet little girl, so lovely, when she was younger. Every boy was sweet around her. Her family, by the rural area standards, were well-up. For some time, she did her schooling at the local school, Nyatate primary school as she stayed with her mother. But she was later transferred to stay with her father in Harare. I used to call her mother, my Mother-In-Law, and greeted her and respected her as a future Son-In-Law is supposed to do, traditionally. Not that I dated the girl then, no. It was just a traditional way to show you appreciate the mother of a beautiful sweet little girl.

She was in her late primary school years when we heard she had been raped by an Uncle whom her father stayed with at their Harare family home. His father had a fall out with this young brother of his, whom he chased away from Harare to come and stay in our local area, again. People thought this Uncle was insane, the village gossiped about this, saying that even the whole family was rather crazy. As she entered her secondary education she started to get absorbed into relationships, one after another. I still called her mother, Ambuya (Mother-In-Law), but it was now because of her little sister that I still respected her. The little sister was also sweet and beautiful. Not that I really did respect the mother. She was a scarlet woman. Later, she was said to be sleeping with her other Son-In-Law, the husband of the younger sister of this girl. That's how bad she was. She stood between her children and their happiness, like a large unwanted present. She had loose control over her girls, seemed to encourage them to misbehave, such that this girl didn't finish her form four as she hitched with a local boy. The local boy who became her husband had nothing, wasn't working, and was looked after by his sisters. The boy's father and mother had died years back such that he made a mess of his life. He got two girls impregnated, at that same time.

He also impregnated another girl from the village to the west of us, in Nyamukapira village. She was a girl I also admired. I thought the guy was stupid, I still think he is, not for the sakes of these two childhood sweethearts he had impregnated. It simply was a stupid thing to do. So, this girl stayed with this boy husband and the girl from Nyamukapira village as a threesome for years, and he burdened her with three kids. The other girl has a number of kids, as well. The boy husband would beat her up and she would run off, returning back home. But after some weeks or months or even in days she will be back with her toy husband. Even when, in most instances, the toy husband never followed on her, she will bite the bullet and return back to the husband's place. For years on end, I heard about this and knew that some day, she will realise it was never meant to be with her.

Her father had since died as she tried all these attempts at a marriage, and her next of kin was that Uncle who had raped her. I wonder what she thought of all that. How the Uncle felt about it all. What had really possessed him, in the first place, to rape his daughter? Now she was her daughter, but I am told he tried to help as best he could, in all these escapades and at one time he had to beat up that toy husband for abusing her. Maybe it was guilt's work.

Eventually, she gave up on the marriage. She packed up her bags and the three kids the toy husband had given her back to her family

20

home, to stay with her prostitute mother. I asked about her a couple of days ago and was told she was back home for the long haul. She is now the mother of this household, her mother has since died of AIDS. That she has now taken to her mother's ways. She is now a prostitute, like her mother. It is a fate she has now embraced. I wonder whether it won't affect her kids, as well as she was affected. Would one of the kids eventually resort to prostitution when life fails her, some years down a lifeline, like her mother, like her grandmother...?

Especially for T

Along comes this lady brimming with all sorts of lovely waves. She is farfillions and farfillions kinds of fineness. We are in Zimbabwe, where a Million things at one time were just as little as a single thing, somewhere in Chitungwiza, and she: Imaging like what I always thought she would… you know, like things from elevated places. My ambition is I want to get my hands on her, to make circles around her, to mould her with my hands, and I deny myself the memory of the last time I got scotched. Fresh (flesh) woman posted to me to soothe my teenage pains. I have been re)awarded her.

We have just gotten here T, and there is always a chance to talk to each other, but I decide to be friends with you, to temper it, to know you better, for you to built trust in me; trust is a plant of slow growths, I had been told. And I reasoned, all love comes from the same soils. Rich, clays, watered, sun-stroked soils and; we have been talking to each other for over a year now.

I now wish I had been writing to you these letters from the start of it all so that now I wouldn't be talking of some of the things in past tense. If it was yester year I could have written you a tone of these letters, me eking out the last few drops of ink to write these letters. Now, I cannot offer you the memory; rather I offer you my love.

And If there is one word, letter, thing I have forgotten to tell you so far is that I am lost and in love with the blazes of your humanity, skins, smiles…, for the darkly flowers unfolding in the heavy shadows of the space around these, and your wide eyes looking trustingly, longingly, believingly into my eyes, lingeringly. Your voice, a smooth bell, calling me from the inside!

Our eyes merely open inside us when we find beauty, and if there is one thing that is the truth, it is that sometimes I don't just know when to say the truth in time, that I stay in yesterday until I find the words to name today. This day:

If rain makes the musics I hear in my heart, what have we made into duets in our soft containers. When you met my music you transcended me into the divine, you made my music extend into you, the strings of my soul flew into your embrace like the edges, urges, rages…, of the summer, our lungs filling up with it to the breaking point, whilst some other times; looking up at that sure, quiet summer blue: My heart wants to dance a storm, to follow the playful steps of a summer dance, to perform a beautiful score.

And the emptiness of our mouths must be filled up with our music, so let's do some calisthenics on our mouths to get our hearts drumming such that when you leave my sight, you leave with something mine inside you, on your mouth, so that we will make new universes, curving new tastes, smells, musics, into it.

Now, the ghosts of us visits me in lonely nights we seem to unleave each other and I have become a sleepwalker patrolling your glowing shores in the dark nights. I contain you in me, like a germ cell Immaculate Conception fetus never to be given birth to. How will I explain it to myself, to you, that I am a nobody but the body of you? What will become you or me then, now that your story is in my body, narrating itself through me? Please, tell me another story, I will write you another letter.

T, this is my home- where love is like logs crackling in a wood burning stove, offering our hearts heat to warm us. T, this is my home, and this is what it's like to see this home through my eyes.

When He Was Far Away From Home

I t had been difficult for him, those past two years, he had been staying far away from home. He spent the first year in Kempton Park. He wasn't going to the church. When he left his home in Zimbabwe, he left under difficult circumstances, for he couldn't take care of himself anymore in Zimbabwe, so he came to South Africa. He was also dealing with a broken down long-term relationship. That year in Kempton Park, almost a year of it, in fact it was 8 months, he stayed with his brother; he had never been to the church. When he left Zimbabwe he was barely going to church, only for the Sunday Mass.

In Kempton Park, he had to take a lift, sometimes two into the city centre where the church was. He had never had to take a lift to church all his life, so he couldn't, but he still kept closer to God, and rarely sinned.

But when he started staying alone in Germiston, he started going to church, after some months there. It was just about one and half kilometres from where he stayed in Delville South. His church was St Augustine Catholic Church, in Germiston South, in Victoria Road as you approach Germiston city centre. The first time he went there, he didn't know which Mass to attend, so he ended up attending the Portuguese Mass, at 8:45, hearing very little that day. And then he was told the English Mass was at 10, so he started attending this English Mass.

That year the church helped him deal with the loneliness, isolation and nonentity of his existence. His life was just about surviving, not living. He had no love, he had no friends. He would listen to Father Rodney's homilies, every week with anticipation. It was not problematic to understand the Father's attitude towards the church, prayer, and Christian life. For over 14 years he had attended Mass in Zimbabwe under the priest with the same disposition on those issues, Father Thomas Fives. So he found resonance with Father Rodney.

One particular Sunday, he was so down after falling in sin, again. It was the same sin that had been troubling him. He came to the church, and he was burdened in guilty. Father Rodney was preaching about sinning that day. Father Rodney said he knew a lot were asking themselves why they should keep coming to the church when they were always sinning, and most of the times, the same sin. He said everyone was a sinner, that everyone sinned. The important thing is to keep trying, to keep giving oneself to Christ, and that one shouldn't give up. The important thing is to keep doing good, helping others.

It reminded him of years back, what he read in an article, on an anthology that was published by Cannongate books, entitled *Writing Wrongs,* in which they were saying that the humans would always fail under sin, but it was better to concentrate one's energies in doing good to others, helping those in need, than concentrating on fighting against sinning. Oh, he recalls well a poem in this anthology from Seamus Heaney. "Human beings suffer/ They torture one another/ They get hurt and get hard/ No poem, or play, or song/ Can fully right a wrong..." He loves Heaney and now with Father Rodney's

26

homilies; he knew he was a normal human being, just suffering in sin, just failing under sin. He was a fallen human being.

The Girl Right Across The Street

She is young, very young to really count for in the world of relationships. She started early, around her grade 6. She was barely 11 then and she was already dating, older guys at that. Her life, from that moment onwards centred on boys, on finding love, as if it's all she was born for. Maybe it was. Her mother got impregnated when she was in Form one, barely thirteen herself. Her grandmother, her mother's mother whom she was staying with, I am told, hitched with a boy in Form two, when barely thirteen herself. When she started dibbling into boys a lot of people in our street said it was expected of her, that she had the same genes as her elders, it was hereditary.

I would talk with her a bit as she entered her Form one class. She was so immersed into relationships, so into boys, and I knew it was a matter of time before she was off the streets into someone's manger. I tried to encourage her to tone down on this hunger for relationships, for boys, for money but it didn't help. And then, midyear, in her Form one year, she went to a party, a couple of streets off ours, at her boyfriend's place and she didn't return home for 3 days. The family, now scared or ashamed, called in Child Support people to get involved. The street was clanging with gossips of her, and everyone called her a Bitch, or Whore or something else bad. Some mentioned the grandmother and mother as the bad influences, their early marriages and said it was expected of her.

She was taken back home, at first by the mother who stays a bit away to tone down the gossips. It seemed she lied to Child Support people that she hadn't slept with the boyfriend, and she also refused to get tested. The boy might have paid off these Child Support people so that they couldn't bring the issue before the law, I don't know. Nothing happened. I knew it was difficult, very difficult for her to face the Street again. Ours is the Rumour Street of the whole Chitungwiza. One has to either let it bother them or just to ignore it.

Eventually, she returned back into the street to stay with her grandmother. She tried to reach out to her friends, to defy the gossip bites behind her back, and she retained most of her social friends, but didn't stop on the boys. After a month or so she was back to basics. She had also been plucked off school by her parents, and someday, I heard the grandmother saying to a friend that she had done enough schooling to be able to write and read for her future husband. When talking to a nearby neighbour, I said the parents should have tried to encourage her to continue with her education, at least that. I said, by removing her from school they were giving her the license to look for marriage or alternatively to be a whore. I think she was at the brink of being the second option. She started visiting night bars, spots, beer halls, and I saw her several times stone-drunk. All she was now interested in was finding a place to lay her head.

As we hit the Christmas period she has disappeared off the streets, again. She has hitched with the said boyfriend or another, we

28

don't know, for sure. The family does not want to talk about her. They lie she is off to school somewhere, but everyone knows it has happened. I hope she will find the place to lay low now and also that in her times of reckless abandon, that she wasn't infected with AIDS. The street as I write this story is ceaselessly clanging with the story of the girl right across the street. Where is the girl, is the question on everyone's lips. The gossips are changeless and primitive; it's like listening to the way a small town would feel after the first real downpour of rain, opening up to the summer.

Plan B

here is a plan B to the World Cup," Uncle Victor says.

"It's FIFA soccer politics," my brother says.

"It's because of Zimbabwe's political situation," I say.

"Guys, the World Cup is good business for everyone," Auntie Florence, Uncle Victor's wife, says.

It is a year away from the World Cup, and the vuvuzelas are being blown into the air to distraction. Some destitute man of our street has made it his plan B, teaching enthusiasts how to blow a vuvuzelas. There is always a plan B to everything in life. I can't run away from home, from the noise, for I have no plan B against these vuvuzelas.

And, in most cases it becomes THE PLAN, I am thinking, I am on my way back from Germiston city centre; one and half kilometre sweet walk to home.

"Hello Bhudhi, there is a job in this white man's place."

"Is it, I am not really looking for a job." I am always scared of strangers thinking they know what I needed, wanted at that moment of contact. But he persisted.

"He is distributing World Cup soccer tee-shirts to kids at a preschool day care. So, this white man needs general hands to help him, and he is paying a hundred bucks."

I could do with a hundred bucks, I thought. I needed a plan B to my depleting cash in my pocket, but I tried to refuse it. It's not safe in the suburb, anymore, especially with the hive of activity around the World Cup. Everyone is looking for a quick buck, but eventually, I agree. This guy who has approached me has also approached another guy who has been walking behind me, all the way from the city centre. I choose to build faith in this safety in numbers.

"The white man wants us to declare everything that we have before we enter into his property, so what do you have, guys."

The other guy who was walking behind me says, "I have a cell and a hundred Rands." He gives these to our benefactor.

"I have 1500 Rands, a cell and these groceries."

Our benefactor says, "Give me the money and cell." And continued,

"The groceries are not a problem." He says as he takes my money and cell.

He leaves us waiting on the front gate of this property, and goes to the side gate, which is in another street. We wait for 3 minutes. It is like an eternity waiting, the weight of an event!

The original plan doesn't always happen, because it is always too ambitious. It strikes me as I run to the other street to check what was taking this guy so long. The street is a clear black of the tarred surface. There is no gate to the property. Blood is exploding in my head as anger surges. I go back to check on the other guy, the guy is nowhere to be found. There is a speeding car in the next street. I could only fold down in the lawns of this property.

31

My uncle is not happy with this, for I have lost him 1500 bucks, but he accepts my explanations. After all, I was plan B. Auntie Florence was away who would do these accounts payments.

But, of course, the World Cup was on-going in South Africa, which was the plan A.

Plan B.

"There is no plan B!" Stepp Blatter refuted what he had blurted out.

The Eagle Prophetess

I was a mere slip of a girl; nobody bothered me, bothered about me, bothered by me. Bothered, I would watch young man, unbothered by me, muscles glistening in the sun, as they left for the hunting grounds, as they came back with the forest's bounty, as *vachitema ugariri-* paying off lobola, through doing chores and tasks at their future In-Laws. The men were busy honeybees, in a field of lavender, none looked my way. I was just a mute orphan, forgotten in luminal spaces. How my heart would beat with longing, wanted to be held, to be told it was right to feel the way I felt. That one day, it would rain on my soul.

Only in my dreams, I would create something, someone who would make me get into the worlds I fantasized about in my day dreams, misspelling my longings. He coloured everything dark, a beautiful fire smoke dark. My dreams made me mad. I could barely breathe; barely close my eyes, awake in my sleeping dreams. Those that the gods blesses…, they first make mad. I was mad, until the moment I opened my eyes, until the moment I started feeling him inside me, like a seed in the soil, bursting with the life of germination.

And afterwards, he never came to my nightmares. I felt like a bed where an animal had slept on for one night.

As I counted the third moon, an icy half circle, I realised I had a seed inside me that had germinated. I told my mother, she told my grandmother. They told me I was pregnant with the demon's seed. They took me away from home. They lied to my father I had to see the old hen prophet. A wise one from a far way kingdom to find my man, that they were accompanying me, halfway to my man. They didn't tell him the truth, that I was cursed. My father would have killed me if he knew the truth, to destroy the demon in me, thereby enveloping the rest of the family in the shadows of the demon. Midway in our secret journey, they abandoned me at the mouth of Chinyamusaka caves, when I was asleep, and when I woke up, I found myself alone. There was no smoke, no drum, and no song.

I knew I had to survive for the sake of the spirit inside me. Thus, I learned to use breathing as a code to keep surviving, to move matter. I knew I was safe as long as I don't harm my pregnancy. I was in the kingdom of the spirit that I knew I carried. I survived, I found all the food I needed every morning when I woke up. In the twelfth month I gave birth to the Me that I had been waiting for. I died in giving birth, but came back into the birth, in my daughter. I could see through myself. Thus instead of my daughter being a monster devil, she would grow up to be a prophetess, and learn the eagle's prophecy. That is the *me* in me that I gave to her. It was not only the hunter's spirit in her but the life-giving spirit she now had. Her destiny was now to save the people, my people, my parents... She had to wait until her time comes to lead her people.

She left the cave as a spirit wind, and was deposited at the Old Hen Prophet's home. The Old Hen Prophet adopted her, even

34

though he felt the quiet shadows in her. The quiet shadows are deals she had made. Not knowing this Eagle Prophetess has a terrible twin, he embraced her. Until the latent twin in the Eagle Prophetess eats the Old Hen Prophet, and takes over, the two stay together.

I also know I didn't give birth to the twin sister of the Eagle Prophetess. It's in my bones that a stranger stepped out of me. I couldn't hold her in my arms, to tame the fierce anger in her darkness. The darkness is impure, implying origin. The Demon liberated her from being born! Whoever is not born does not die? Or was I afraid if I birthed her, the three of us would die. She was taken away in the moment of my death, before I had returned into the Eagle Prophetess' spirit, by the Demon that had raped and impregnated me in my dreams. Deep into Chinyamusaka cave, across the borders of infinity, to be trained into her dark brood. Gifted with sight, yet still remaining completely in the dark. No day now is safe from the darkness of her; this baby of mine is the Vulture Prophetess. Until she murders the Eagle Prophetess, leave a message for me written in her blood, I don't know where she is now. How to un-love her, my refugee, my peace, my freedom, my prison! She is the funeral of my soul.

PART 3: A CONVERSATION

And then

She tells him she wants his mouth to find her other mouth.

The Promises Of Love:
(with re-imaginings of the story, "Sunset")

Your love mirror

You stare and stare and it stares back at you. You laugh and it laughs back at you. You also know that whatever it is, it is feeling the same things that you are also feeling. You aren't blocked. You aren't disturbed. You feel yourself entering into it. You are stuffing it up with all the things that you are feeling.

You lock *her* in your arms. You close the world down. You fold time in. You also kill things from sheer curiosity here! You know you are also making an unconscious effort not to keep staring at this image. You can't close your inner eyes though. They keep staring at this image that is now deeply embedded inside you. She has become faith to you.

Love

This is the surname you have forgotten but its memory still lingers in your mind's soft strands. Prismatic colours of this (your) second name, are bursting into touches. Every meaning, shadow-touches of her hands, is an endless rehearsal- a session, a jam... You feel her hands on you even when she is not there with you. It is your skin, the biggest interlocutory organ of your body! It is so alive like a pointillist painting: that from far away looks so well knitted, seamless. Your passion for her is an endless landscape of Omega. You also have discovered that this love is now your accomplished existences, bursting through in lyrical bubbles. Singing a re-echoing the world of flooding gaps. It is a song that has lulled you to sleep, it is an open sky and the rains are falling down on you. You let them rain down on you boy! So this love of yours has survived: the face of man in what is the beginning, the heavenly, Alpha? You recall the memories of exploding into this relationship; photo (eye)-tactical, water (star)-sweepings, tongue (finger)-kissings, ebbing away, like waves on the beach. You recall the shacking off of love's final shivers: traces in the wind of your last kisses with Patricia, thoughts of her keep swimming up your mind, like an insistent fish that keeps mouth-hitting your legs

38

in search of (for) food; sometimes like unseen scrawny insects across your skin, in the black holes of your mind.

The language of love

Engaged by these musical resonances of the language of love, and relying on the tricks of your mind always getting you home, you have bought into this marriage thing. For the two years you have been seeing the other, your mind has spread out; away from you, has no more plain symbols, charts or helpful indexes. The last summer lumbered to its inevitable end, the way a song modulates from minor to major chords. Achieving dissonance, consonance, and harmony, and then dying in the listener's ears, she like the previous summer has already left, without your noticing it. She has no more plans for you this winter, but you have continued to believe in your love for her, even when her perfume has wafted into the thin blue air and the magic has died down? Unless you know the quality of your soil: these seeds of your errors can creep upon the path of your feelings. Your small stories already wondering away, and the only story could be the one that lies ahead....

The eye of a bull

This week of waiting has been a bothersome one. It has been tarnished by cumuli-nimbo-strato clouds of your mind's clouds infested skies. You seemed like you were sited in the middle of the tip-tilting sky; the quivering suns and the bursting bright blue stars. This week you have also dissected the eye of the bull with your surgeon-brained, thought knives. You have also discovered that the bull was not fully pregnant. Like us, demons also study the silent spaces of our lives. She phoned you last week: telling you that she is done with you. You remember you had said to her that you had heard of that before, that you had used that several times when you were the uninterested, the (unconvinced) one. You also told her that she had become a network against your feelings. You had also asked to see her. She said she would see you in a week's time. You hadn't been bothered by that mountain against your feelings throughout the week- that network against your feelings; for you thought you had already mounted it. To be stubborn can encompass a mountain of stupidity too. But you couldn't help thinking; thinking the entire week about which soldiers were now on Patricia's side, making love to her! And which were on your side, what uniforms were they wearing? It seemed all the soldiers were now wearing the same uniform, Patricia's uniform.

Mocking you, laughing at you, gorging those new wound-sites of yours with their swords, with her words!

Patricia

She tells you it's over again. Patricia says "no" to you and takes flight to the next yard, to the next human prospect, to the next sex prospect, to the next love prospect, to the next... You have also discovered that it is too late: that she can take things away from you without a wink. Like the rain when it paters away, taking things away with it; but also leaving some things behind. What's wrong Patricia? You ask her and she answers you using words. Nothing José. But you are all beyond the words you are using. There is only rhythm to the sound that is propelling you to use words. Your rainbow of happiness arches and arches and arches..., half is falling this way in the slathers of your anguish, and another half is falling that way to the hill. That half then falls behind the hill is like a half frown, like the colours of a childhood painful smile. These dances of lively rhythms are thoughts; thoughts rich in un-speech; like the silent mad siren. You are so pink and raw. This rawness is stretching the tensions in the brittle chains of your thoughts. Happiness can be a dying mayfly!

Pain-sites

Most of the days of your affair with her you had just got on together by license. In the beginning when you believed there was hope in the relationship, somehow inside her she had known there was nothing, but she hadn't told you that, rather she kept turning you into new curves and false promises. You had seen all these half-lights and shadows, the evasions and denials but she kept telling you lies. But you also knew she had been lying to you because she had said all those excuses and lies as if telling the truth was as simple. Everything came to a hurtful par on a hurtful August afternoon. The previous night you had made love to her at her place for the first time and it was good and you agreed with her that you could move in with her and try your luck at a marriage later. But that day you had woken up and went to college and it was your first year at the University of Zimbabwe. You were so full of purple thoughts on love and a light that was neural enclosed you. But when you arrived at the campus there was a strike raging-on with the police already cordoned around the campus refusing everyone entrance in and out of the campus and so you had returned back to your lodgings heightened by that emotional awareness that could only crush into depression, packed your things and in the calm of the late afternoon sun you were at her lodgings. What you saw that day twisted your heart. She had another man and they were abandoned into lovemaking. You had never made an effort to get to know about pain before, but from that day onwards you became bloody-brothers with pain and much of your time after that was spent in trawling through pain-sites and checking wound-sites and trying to recognise if they were getting any better, or not. You had met her some couple more times and by the end of that year she disappeared and months later you heard that she died.

Dead!

Just like that!

She had died on you!

Grandmother

Said to you that death; life and renewal leave something else behind, an indelible mark, a memory of a time and place, a sweet taste. A time you were together with someone! She said that no matter how much deleting that takes place, that there are always shadow impressions, forms lurking and emerging in the dark. She also said that death is like the water throwing away its own soul to be carried away only as liquid, a muddy liquid after a rainy day, clogging everything, only the muddy, only the pain that you are feeling. She said that we deserve nothing in life other than the fraction of a second that we get in taking the next breath; that we are assured of nothing other than hoping and lying to ourselves that we have all our lives to live. She also said we are always given a lifeline, a very precious lifeline that should be lived for the good of the life-giver, that we can do a whole lot good with that chance and that we can make it the happiest moment of our lives. She also told you that there are some people who have been living with the disease that you had, that they know they are going to die and when isn't important to them but how to live well their almost assured life and that maybe most of us who don't have the disease you have might die before you.

Portraits in the darkness

You know you have been blown by this hope that your grandmother talked of into the next time zone like those things that comes up like portraits in the darkness. What man can measure and define the darkness in his heart? You also know that some of these portraits in darkness, you can learn to deal with. That it's like for you to get through life you really have to let go some of these things, especially those that hurt so bad. Of course you know that it's not only lovers who get this disease. That it is like cancer, like autism. That it is a pervasive disease and that it affects whole families. It would be like the whole family has it. But grandmother also told you that if you have believed that what you have believed in was deeply rooted in the truth that you didn't have to give up, even if it meant standing alone, or threatening your very existence.

The language of the truth

But you let this story breathe itself out. You let the story write itself in the language of the truth to your grandmother, but also in a language of double helixes of this truth to yourself. You tell your grandmother that your life is now a house unbuilding itself. The builders abandoned it summers ago amidst construction, and never returned to finish it. Every season has found its mark on this house, eroding it, breaking it down. Not to forget people, whores who transact in it, kids who play hide and seek in it, the drunkards who pisses, shits in it, the animals who can't be outdone by the humans! It is a life in which you have raked what was dead from the ground, displaced it, but lost a bigger part of yourself in the detritus? That the debt you had incurred was payable only one way. The cherry to garnish this cocktail was only one. Like the baptism in the Jordan you know there is no half-way to it but only full immersion. That you could only become the person your grandmother was talking of but that it would be with a little curtsy...

The shadows

The shadows around you are like those of Geje, those of Misheck, those of that little girl and that other man who killed himself when he discovered he was HIV positive. That man stayed in the adjacent village and the little girl in her early secondary school years. That a family man could tell his family that he was going to kill himself, leave home, wife and kids and ran away in the middle of the night and go to a distance of over twenty kilometres in the thick forests of Muchena, east of your village, besides Hunyani river and commit suicide by hanging himself! Your mother told you those people were possessed of evil spirits. She told you that nobody should mourn for them, that they would go straight to hell and that nobody had to talk about them because to talk about them was to invite their bad spirits back. That was difficult for you to understand for years; especially why Misheck thought it was better to die than to live. You had grown up with all these things like your shadow and you couldn't help thinking about them whenever you heard someone had committed suicide.

…. like the footfalls of the dark clouds)

(The footsteps of black smoke:

….To be eaten by Geje)

To know the mind of that man, that girl….

.... (To accept Misheck)

Misheck

Some people thought Misheck deserved a break and that it was meant to be, that at least he had finally found some rest, at last. It was a little bit encouraging to know that in some people's minds they wanted Misheck to find rest, but you also knew a lot of people still thought otherwise, including your mother. Misheck had come from a very poor family. His father Geje and this name had come about because whenever he was greeted, *Good morning,* he always replied, "Geje, geje, bho, bho, bho," which meant, "alright, alright, fine, fine, fine," so he was called Geje. Geje was a local builder, a binge beer drinker. The monies he got from his construction concern were spent in drinking himself into a stupor. His children, including Misheck barely made it and the mother had borrowed a lot for the upkeep of this family, let alone for their school fees which she had paid for by doing some little jobs like cultivating and weeding other people's fields.

Drinking himself to death

Geje eventually had a leg amputated. He had burned the leg in a fire when he was drunk at a traditional beer ceremony in the village. They said he had passed out drunk and that he had been asleep near a fire. That he had put his leg onto the fire. Some people said, jokingly, that Geje thought his leg was a log of wood so he wanted to rekindle the fire with his leg. Some said that he had been trying all his life to kill himself like his child Misheck, and that, that was another suicidal attempt. He was wearing plastic gumboots so the gumboot caught fire and he had lost the leg because it had taken a lot longer for people to remove it from his burning leg. When it was removed his leg was destroyed and was insensate such that the Doctor had to cut the biggest chunk of the leg upto the underpants position. Geje had become a wreck on cripples, following the village's beer trail and drinking himself to death...

Geje's death

It had taken a week of waiting for people to pronounce him truly dead and the rumours that had abounded that week. People were saying that he was dying and coming back from the dead inside a day, that is, he will be dead and cold in the evening but warm, breathing and very much alive the following morning, only to die and arise from the dead in the next twenty four hours. When they finally certified him truly dead you were so afraid of him such that you had refused to attend his funeral. You couldn't be there for Misheck who had come home from his workplace for his father's funeral. You were so scared of the stories of some Tokoloshis; the half-human, half-animal monsters people were saying were the things that had taken hold of Geje's life and being. These Tokoloshis, people said were the things that had been refusing to die not Geje who had been dead for over a week. They said that when those Tokoloshis had finished drinking Geje's blood that's when those things had left his body. Some people said they were at Geje's home waiting and looking for someone to take hold of. You were so scared of attending the funeral because you were so scared they would get into you and drink you to death like they had done to Geje, and for a year you refused to go to Misheck's place.

Suicide

This night though, and for the first time your Mother had talked about Misheck and for the first time in years you have come to the conviction that Misheck had done the best thing there was, and that killing oneself was a better option, sometimes. Your mother talking about Misheck had galvanised this all the more because it meant there was nothing wrong with killing oneself or talking about someone who had committed suicide. But are you really going to commit suicide, or you just want to cleanse yourself of the disease, of the pain, of everything that had gone wrong in your life? You also tell yourself that you have to pay for not being a good friend to Misheck, for all the other suicides that you had heard of and accepted as good, but you also know that you are going to meet up with all these people, that you are going to tell them that you now understand how they felt and why they killed themselves. You can't also help thinking of them now as you are making your way to the Mutsatsati tree. The only thing that bothers you is that some people might never really understand the way that you are feeling now, the way that you now understand how Misheck felt those many summers ago. But you also know it's Misheck you have to obey this time and he is calling for you to come over to him. It is his voice that you hear.

At the grave place

But you also don't expect this ghastly stillness that blankets the rows of tombs near this Mutsatsati tree. You also remember there is this Chinese tradition you have heard of- of burning paper money at funerals. You know it wouldn't suffice for you. What the hell would one do with that shit ash; buy an ash-cell phone, an ash-car, an ash-house, an ash-husband, an ash-wife for yourself, an ash-HIV positive status for you on the other side of the grave, maybe! Ashes to the a(sses(hes! Only the gods knows the exact nature of the devil that had you infected with this disease. *Patricia.* Who was already ashes, and you were ashes, you have to return to ashes, to your original soil form. They say beauty is on the inside but this is where hate resides, lost in the deepest recess of one's mind and when set out; only a shell of what we were is what would be left. What kind of species that would pulp its own, and then grinds life and love to ashes like that? Humans! Death, it made you remember your grandmother telling you about life, death and renewal at your brother's funeral. Your grandmother also said to you that parts of us are never removed, erased or forgotten but rather that each of these creates some other wholes and leave impressions that couldn't easily be wiped away. And, as you are trying to deal with the pain around your neck from the rope around your neck, you remember your grandmother who had raised you, whom you had stayed with. Such a sweet old lady she was.

Leonard

He was twenty three years old, when he finished his 'O' levels, five years before. With so much hope of getting a good job, he had moved to the city of Harare, *H-Town*. That's where most young hopeful man would move to after school, in search of brighter prospects. In the first days in this city he could spend the whole odd day, patrolling, more like a soldier the industrial streets, hunting for a job. He had done all that he could, and here and there, behind closed doors, people with relatives, people who could bribe the foreman were taken in. He didn't have money to pay for a taxi into the industrial area from his high density township suburb of Glen Norah, he had walked everyday to the industrial areas, then let alone money to bribe the marketplace-souled foreman.

They wanted to have more and more. If you give them money in exchange with employment, it won't end there. At your first payday they would be expecting more, and at your next paydays some more and more. It would continue like that. It was the suk-mentality- it was the mosquito's suk-mentality, and it had sunk deep roots into the whole fibre of the society. Leonard knew he had to either dance to its tune or face a cold stomach every night, but he couldn't bring himself to do that yet. He had told himself that one day things would look up for him.

But for five years he had walked every road surface of the industrial areas, the city centre, the residential areas and nothing good came out of it. Thus a few days before Christmas of his twenty third year, he bed his widowed aunt farewell. He couldn't keep burdening her anymore, draining the little she earned from selling fruits, vegetables and other small wares on the streets. She had two school going children to look after, as well. It was chaotic to raise money for these children's school fees, let alone for their daily upkeep.

Leonard had returned back home, to his struggling, live by the hands, toil all day long parents who were still farming a spent up plot of six acres and a garden patch by the river. He was shattered. He felt betrayed by the kind of life he had met up with in the bright diamond lighted city of Harare. Only home, in the far backward black water rural setting could help sooth his benumbed feelings and cold hopes. He had helped his family doing the weeding and many other field jobs at their family. When the crops had come toward harvesting, that's when everything, his life, his hopes and feelings had taken another dangerous spiralling turn.

Leonard was coming from the local shops, Chirowamhangu shopping centre, going home in Sharamba village, tucked in the banks of the Nyajezi River, where he stayed. He had been send, by his mother, to procure their thin grocery of kapenta fish, 750ml bottle of cooking oil, 500 grams of salt at Chirowamhangu shops. He had met Mr. Karidza, who stayed at Hogo village, to the north of Sharamba village, a couple of villages from Sharamba. He had heard a lot about Mr. Karidza and his associations with the newly formed political party, Democratic Alliance Labour Party. Mr Karidza was its chairman for the Nyanga constituency. It turned out Karidza, a friend of their neighbour Mr. Maboreke, was going to his friend's place, to discuss with Mr. Maboreke his possibility of taking over the chairmanship of the Sedze cell, after the incumbent of that seat had been killed in political motivated violence. Karidza was an affable frank man in his late fifties. He had no children of his own, so any young person was always special to him.

He knew how to befriend young people who would pass for his kids, if he had any. He found in these young people the kids he never got; they had failed to conceive in their marriage. These two, Leonard and Karidza had talked about life in the city of Harare, life in the whole country, life in their area, the failures and progress of the whole country, how and when things had gone wrong, and their hopes now. This had become the first time since his returning from Harare that Leonard had been able to talk to anyone, how he felt and had fared in Harare. What hopes he still had for himself? There was this way in which Karidza seemed to unlock Leonard's inner self and make him pour his heart out, his fears, his frustrations and his hopes. Somehow he didn't find it unthinkable when Karidza offered him the constituent's leadership of the youth league of DALP. It simply was the correct thing to do.

This had given birth to the satisfaction he now felt as he walked along the road to Nyatate service centre. He had used the central road to Nyatate because it was the nearest way to reach Nyatate. He had a meeting to catch up with in Dandadzi village, just a stone's throw from Nyatate Service Centre. This road was also safe because it snaked through people homes. There was little possibility of getting abducted by the thugs of the other party, Jongwe party, who were terrifying, beating and kidnapping people into submitting to this

55

party, especially in the Sanyabako and Tenga villages, where the other road to Nyatate would go through.

Their meeting came to an early end that day, due to five youths from Tenga village who were making unnecessary disturbances and interjections, throwing rowdy statements and threatening everyone there, promising everyone at the meeting a beating if they continued attending it. These youths, Thomas, Arnold, Christopher, Taurai and Paul had been to school with Leonard, at the adjacent Nyatate Secondary School, 5 years before, but they were not quiet friends with Leonard, even during school years. These were from Jongwe party and were the ones who had been abducting, killing and beating up people in their constituency. These disturbances had forced the Nyatate branch chair, Mr Guta, to call for the disbanding of the meeting before its actual stretch.

Something wasn't right, somehow. Leonard felt it in his bones, as he trudged in the autumn dusk back home. There was something in his bones that screamed something he didn't seem to hear, telling him to seek shelter in the homes he was passing through in the Magaya village, the last village before his Sharamba village. He disdained it. He was almost home. He told himself he was just scared because it was night and he was entering a stretch of forest that had no homes. It was far away from Nyatate so he told himself he had no fear of those youths from Jongwe party, who had stayed behind in their village, Tenga village, which was next to Dandadzi village, to the other side of Nyatate centre.

As he crossed Nyajezi River he saw some fun shadow ahead of him, so he stopped and tried to look hard in the darkening night, but couldn't make what it was. Then, he heard the whooshing sound of

56

something flying towards him. He thought it was a bird so he ducked a bit, thinking it would miss him, but before he finished ducking he was hit, blinded by that duck, on the forehead. It was a stone and, he collapsed on the bridge and fainted.

They beat him with all sorts of traditional weaponry, rods, sticks, axes, pangas, cutting into his flesh. They cut him into pieces and defecated on his pieces and left him dead. Leonard was discovered by the first bus driver that used that road, which plied Nyatate to Harare route, cut into pieces, by the side of the road, off the bridge.

Running/ Snakes/ Tsunamis/ Mountains...

We had been running, up, up the terrain, up the mountains. The mountains curl above everything else like an animal in mid pounce. They define us, and by contrast as we run towards them, we exaggerate their majesty to temper our poor reflections. Behind the sea is now a huge monster mountain chasing us, as well? We are in the middle of these two mountains. This water behind us, chasing us, is rising up the terrain to gobble this mountain, and ahead of us; we have to negotiate our way around falling avalanches of mountains, landslides, broken trees, and rocks- flying like wafts of feathers in light wind. I am with my cousin, and someone else, I don't know him. We are running away from this ocean swelling with a huge tsunami mountain.

Snakes, Snakes, Snakes...

I am coming off from my Auntie's place, in our little village Mapfurira, going back home, when I try to take our cattle home to the kraals. They are in the fields of some cousin's plot, but snakes start sprouting from everywhere. Some look like our snake, a long snake I have known almost all my life, which stays in the hedges by our next door neighbour, my cousin's hedge yard. People of our village call it our snake, so we have learned to adopt it as ours, even though the hedges belong to my cousin. A colourful brownish reddish snake, and now it seems, it has created, I don't know by what process, different kinds of progenies by every turn I take, as I try to avoid their bite-some fangs.

I see Hoop snakes biting their tails and rolling like wheels down the flowing gradient. Then I see a copperhead snake, off some mountains to the west, I suppose. And I turn my head to the east, I see two black racers and I don't know from which burns they have come from, hissing speed and terror in my heart. From the south, and I suppose from the river, I see water moccasins. We were told by grandma these would dominate creeks and were said to enter people through their anus. If they enter you they could only be killed inside your body by committing incest, by sleeping with your own sister on top of the thatched kitchen roof whilst everyone watches, waits. I have to really avoid these ones, I tell myself. Then to my left side I see pit vipers, a bunch of them striking the earth like some blind man fumbling with locks, until the ground around them turn red from their blood. Then, off these vipers, are timber rattlers shaking dead man's bones in their fearsome sound. And I have to negotiate myself around all these snakes!

In the dream it reminds me of when we were little; somewhere in grade 3, at Nyatate primary school. We had to negotiate our way through the python snakes, all over the grounds surrounding the adjacent Nyatate secondary school. These, though, didn't want to bite us.

It was because a white expatriate teacher at this school had captured a python snake he had found in the mountains surrounding this place, and tried to tame it to make it his playing-with-mate. He removed its teeth and poison, and the previous Wednesday, he had brought it back to this school, doing a snake show with it. We had attended that show, but afterwards, python snakes started sprouting from all over, blocking our paths from and to school. We had to jump them on our way to this school. It seems to be the situation with me now. But, I haven't done any sacrilege to this place. The place of my birth is ruled by the Wanyama people, who are of the python snake totem, so pythons and my own totem- The Lion- which is the spirit medium of this place, are sacred beings. Nobody is allowed to kill these. If you kill these, it would cause sacrilegious happenings. But, in the dream I haven't killed anyone.

Is it because; I am coming from the funeral. I was at a funeral, but I am not even sure anymore who had died, at my Auntie's place. Maybe, it is my uncle who had passed on, some few months before. Maybe, I am trying to process his death. But, I am not the one who killed him, so I don't know why these snakes want to bite me. I succeed, as eventually, they give up on trying to bite me and run down by the middle of my cousin and our yard, looped together, and it seems with some of our cattle, looped around our cattle. It's a huge tread and the noise that they make!

I only have two beasts with me, the rest have been gulped in by our snake. I get to our home's gates, and I let the two beasts proceed to the kraals on their own, for they know their way. I wake up from this dream as I enter our place. When you wake up from a dream and then later start dreaming another one, it's as if that time between is now a void time.

Tsunamis, Tsunamis, Tsunamis...

I am determined to survive the tsunami, for surviving has become my new Buddha. We get to a high mountain, which we seek shelter in. Somehow, deep in myself, I tell myself it is now safe, but things are falling down this mountain, spilling all over, leaping off like a cat on top of a hot oven. I am holding onto a strong branch of a tall tree. Eventually everything is tranquil. A tranquil after a devastating battle, knowing it might start all over again.

We alight from this mountain, and start running again, up the higher land and mountain range as everything starts sibling with anger, again. The redbird and bluebird in the grass are two phones away from each other. The land looks like the Cape area, in South Africa, and then it looks like we are in South East Asia, somewhere in the Philippians, Thailand..., somewhere in the lands of the tsunamis. It's a landscape I can barely recognise, some other times.

The Wolf Cousin

I am still running, and we get to a white farming area in the mountains. At the first farm we reach, this cousin of mine grabs a hen, and I tell him he is stealing. He should let go the chicken. That we have to find the owner to ask for food, but he is adamant that we should kill this hen and eat it uncooked. I try to grab the chicken from him; he becomes a gnarled wolf, flanging his teeth at me, raising his claws with which I thought he might scratch out my eyes. I shiver with terror as he gorges his nails into his own flesh, scooping this blood in his hands and licking it like ice cream. I feel so hungry I want to drink my own blood, too, but I start running away from this thought, and the thought thinks, I am running away from this wolf cousin, but this wolf cousin changes back into human form. Have I decided of this wrongful dream turn to fill in the dark times of nightmare territory of that tsunami fast approaching us? One thought becoming the next by dream! I don't know. I keep running, dreaming. I can't stop because I know the ocean is making its way to me. It has swallowed a lot of people.

The Internet Café

When I started having the premonition that something is going to be wrong, I was at the Internet Café Shop I frequently used at Zengeza 4 Shopping Centre, trying to access and work on my mail. I had been trying to access my accounts, but failing. The hot electric bulb burning straight as erections, talking, whispering, telling me...

Don't dream, don't dream, don't dream....

At one time I ask for help from Chris, the attendant of this café but nothing happens, and I am so anxious to access my emails. There is a letter that explains everything in my Yahoo mail account. The internet café is in the first floor, so I take the steps down, and then my brain tells me something is wrong. I tell people who are near me that something is wrong. It is like in the movie, *Final Destination, 5*. But with all these people, it's like the sort of dream one tries to leave but their limbs won't respond. They don't believe me, so I start running. A number of people run with me, but a few make it across the bridge of the river across this Internet Café Shop, and the rest are taken in by this river, as it swoons with the water from the ocean.

Running, Running, Running...

We get to the next place, a Chinese man's place, who is busy trying to secure his cattle against this monster tsunami. I ask him for food. He wants to give me something and is looking around for something. When my cousin comes hard on heels behind me, and behind him, is a white man, the owner of the hen he had stolen. The white man starts accusing us, me and my cousin, of stealing. He takes his hen. This Chinese man who wanted to give me something to eat tells me to leave his property, or else he is going to shoot us. We start running away from this place. I can't stop running even though I am so hungry.

We get to a place where they are groups, two groups of people, fighting each other. I don't even know what the fight is all about. I am forced to help those to the side in which we came into this fighting. We fight. Whilst we are fighting, it seems I haven't stopped running up the mountains.

I get to the third place, and at this place there is this racistic angry (black) man. He is bullish, and fierce. He reminds me of the lion we saw a week before the snakes starting sprouting all over Nyatate grounds. A lion, walking in broad daylight, in the main roads from the Muchena Mountains, through Nyatate villages, going all the way to Turo Mountain and, this was the lion that was the spirit medium of the Wanyama tribe, heralding the coming of the snakes.

The Lion

It was so sure of itself as it treads its land. It, just being there, was threatening enough, even though we knew it was harmless, and wouldn't eat us. This ~~black~~ man is as threatening. I ask him for food, but he points his riffle at me and releases the trigger. I am hit by the chest by a hot bullet. I tell myself that I am dead. Someone, that other guy we were with, somehow kills this ~~black~~ man. But, he also gets killed, as well. I am seeing all this, yet I thought I was dead. I did not get killed by the ~~black~~ man. I feel like I have been assimilated into his culture and made the king. I rise from my death's position, and start running again.

I am fighting in several group wars, a war for survival. I manage to jump to the other side, as my cousin and everyone else fighting in these group wars are taken in an avalanche of the ground by the ocean. I hear muddy death screaming all over, wringing, and climbing towards me. I start running fast off this ocean, up the ranges of mountains.

Up The Mountains

I am running as I see a car with people in it being taken down the terrain into the all consuming ocean. It's now huge springs that are sprouting all over the mountains ahead of me- that are dangerous and creating whirling furling rivers down the mountains. I have to avoid these springs, as I run up these mountains. I see some people with a traditional cart, going up this mountain. They are not friendly nor enemies. They don't see me, even if they are seeing me. I don't care, I am running. In me, I know I have to get on top of these ranges of mountains to be safe from the ocean. But, I know I have to go the other side of these mountains to be really safe, because it gets told in me that these mountains, at any moment, are going to sprout into volcanic lava. It's the larger fear for me to avoid this eventuality. So I am determined as I run hard. I know I am going to be the only survivor from all this. I don't feel angry. I don't feel triumphant. I don't feel sad. I am emotionless, as I wake up from this dream.

WhatsApp Love

In the dream he is like a train that has lost its tracks in the mountainous eastern highlands of Nyanga. He starts rolling down the slope, jaggedly rolling, hits several stone boulders, bumps higher and harder into air. He hits the slopes, rolling off like a huge thing, breaking into pieces on his way down, until he hits the valley river, cools down in the river...and when he wakes up, it's the couple of nights before dream that he remembers.

The birds, off the school yard he is staring at are exploding with song, a song of the blooming flowers and leaves of early spring. It is a mildly hot day, the breeze; a sweet rootless breeze makes waves, sweet waves on the trees and grass. It is a school yard he has used, over the years to cool his hot mind. When it gets too hot upstairs he would hag the durawall to this school grounds and watch the semi natural world. He wishes the football pitch and goalposts were not there- it would be an untamed wilderness, but this place always gets him, gets him through anything. He is not even sure what the magic of this place is.

It had also become involved with his subconscious, in a way he is trying to understand too. He had dreamt, a couple of nights before, he had entered these grounds. He went all the way to the school buildings, beyond the school buildings, and out through the gate in Mubvumira road. He travels a bit further, and then something makes him start returning back. He is now with this girl he has loved for a month now, who has recently ended it with him. It was the usual

69

reason, his age. He was 40 that year, and she was twenty one. He thought he could let her know earlier on how old he was. It's always a conflicting world that love invokes in him. Part of his heart would be telling him it's not his to have- that part has the knack to get in the way, forcing its way, most of the times. Another part wants to give in- to be overwhelmed. It always gets overpowered by the part that wants to crumple things. So, eventually, it had gotten its way. That part thought it could use age and no one will blame it, knowing also it would create a world he was unhappy. He was the master at unhappiness! He had the fucking degree to prove it! Well, and over 40 years experience!

There had been together for a month. She was blooming into something beautiful and it had started tagging some beautiful things in him. When he told her about his age she was overwhelmed.

They had started a long way off this discussion. They had been talking of how reluctant to talk she had been, and that she was now communicating well. She said,

"You asked a lot questions. You know, it's difficult to start talking to someone you don't know much about, and you are not used to, worse still, when you have only met him online."

"Yes, I know..., it was difficult for me too... So I figured if I talked a lot then I am sure to always have something to say or explore, if I am bereft of things to say." Then he talked of how it was difficult to say how he felt about her. She teased him,

"Yes, it's you who was scared", and then she laughed, "I don't bite!"

Out of nowhere he said, "I have one leg."

"What is wrong with your other leg?"

"Burned to a stamp in a fire."

70

"Please, say the truth." He knew she was bothered, already. Then he threw in the real issue he wanted to talk to her about.

"And, I am also older than you."

"It's obvious!"

"Are you comfortable with that?"

She joked that she thought the leg had been cut off by the husband of a wife he had had an affair with...

They laughed together, "...*kkkkkk*" "*kkkkkk*", and then she asked him.

"How old are you, really?"

"40", there it was out and then he continued, "Nopes, I am joking about the leg, but I am 40, never been married though."

"*Hahahahahahahaha....*", She laughed for a long time, more like the real laughter, not online laughter, "*kkkk, kkkkk*"; sobered and asked.

"Where is your wife? Don't tell me you haven't been married before."

"That's what I have just said, no kids. I am alone." He knew he was already alone. She was going.

"There might be a lot of stories behind your back for you to get here without marrying."

"Not many," he had laughed to ease the feeling of loneliness enveloping him. "I was just pursuing my dreams, wasn't ready to commit to a serious relationship, yet."

He couldn't tell her there was a time he was committed, nine years before, but that she had crushed his world and turned it upside down. That, for nearly a decade, he was dealing with that. It's a "story"- he had said there were no stories behind his back, so he couldn't tell her that.

71

"I didn't feel I was mature. I think I would have messed it and her, as well..., and there are no other stories."

"*Hoooooooo*...but now, *oooo*, my God! You took too long to come to this. Who knows what else you were doing all along."

It was this that had thrown him off and put him on the edge. He realised that he liked her a lot, even though he hadn't meet her. Now she was leaving him. They always leave; it must be a huge thing to deal with, his age. She hadn't come around to it afterwards. He had tried to explain to her it doesn't matter. She was afraid of conventions. She said she was the last born in her family of five. The oldest of whom was 36, 4 years younger than he was. It is this that troubled her. He even told her of how he had lost his previous girlfriend through the same problem. Eventually, he told her he had argued his case. It's now up to her to figure out what is the right thing to do.

"You can decide to say, 'no', its fine, really..., I will understand... I can't change that about me... I am so sorry."

It was the loser, the brutaliser, the unbelieving him, that would say things like that. It had accepted that she was lost. She stalled a bit.

"You know, I can't decide now."

"I know, but don't take too long, hey!"

It was just something he had to say but he knew she would be back very soon with a, "No!"

She was the following morning.

"I have decided we can't be together. I am really sorry." Then it was over, was it...

So, for weeks he had dealt with shit. He knew he was disturbed when he had that dream. In returning back, he had passed through the school grounds, which were now riven by galleys of water flowing off. These were not threatening like the usual rivers of his dreams, but they were so many. It was an odious task to deal with each gulley. He was with her, but she was not really her. But he knew she was, in his bones. Yet, it was someone else. At least they were negotiating their way together, on their way through the galleys. The girl was with a young child now, and then he woke up to the sound of a child crying. It was just the next door kid belting her early morning prayer.

For the biggest part of the week he had felt empty, painful and bereft of feelings. He had been transferring the pain around, on him, on others. Then, he realised what he was doing, so he stopped talking to people, and enclosed himself inside. Inside he has a place he feels safe, finds serenity. He started watching movies, one after another. Cooked, ate, bathed and then watched some more movies. He didn't want to feel unused. He knew it would drive him crazy.

Their Marriage:
with re-imaginings of the story, "RUINS."

She had to talk to him

She is thinking to herself that it might really take the shiver of notes of a consort of foghorns for her to sound the cool depths of this still pond. She is watching for a tickle of wind on this water's skin as a reminder to tell her of the sadness of all that had gone wrong with this man. He doesn't show her by any visible outward signs that he is aware of her or any other passengers. Droplets of words gathers at her lips, refusing to suck the nature out of all that is deeper inside her, a powerful current stronger than the subtler opening of her mouth. She simply knows she has to talk to him. Here will be some few words that due to their utterance, consumes old things and shed new things, leaving traces of things that had not been there in the first place.

She knew she had to talk to him!

Be-Longing

after reading Jenna Mervis' poem "Shedding Skin."

It takes the two many solid years of dating to think about everything. It should now be the right decision. Time has made it the right decision, and she really deserves it. She has been there for him. Life is threaded in belonging and ends up *swaddled in belonging: One's life in relation to someone's life, a wife's life in relation to the husband's life, a girlfriend's life in relation to a boyfriend's life. One's death in relation to someone's death, bones in the grave in relation to the soil or a person's spirit. Someone's soul in relation to the endower or to the devil or even to nothingness. Even life in between is swaddled in belonging. Belonging to someone is the icon of our connections that have made museums of all our memories and shaped us into individuals! Belonging to someone is the signs that have mapped the man-made marriages of our past. Our lives and our futures, too!*

Be-Longing to someone is not BELONGING to someone!

Parallel Environments

Burned, scared and full of fear he had turned to her. And for as long as he now remembers she has become the rain into his life, raining tender flowers of water to cool his heart. *Who cares about that, whiner? Let's start with the lady's side of the coin!*

1. On her side she only knows she has to marry him like we all know that once we are born what's left is to die. It should be there and then or else tomorrow might bring in another complication and one doesn't want to kick *h(ier)my-self* where it hurts the most. *Stop complaining, I have made it a word!*

2. She has come a long way and she is prepared to go so much more further to make their life together a beauty. *So, she says!*

3. To him, his life now is an oasis calmed inside the edges of this love; it is still-stopped. It now exists inside the world of this love. *Okay, its okay...*

4. *But most of the time we are just parallel dreams..., parallel environments, that's how very little we know of the other whilst what we ever loved in the other becomes a blurred pixel in the warning horizon.*

5. *And in one lifetime a hundred lives can pass through us. Sometimes we just watch these lives passing through us, each a tug at a lifeline, hardening the heart's landscape.*

So that we become ourselves at one remove!

Blindfold Identity

*C**ould this be because we have been blinded by the too bright rays of love or it's because we have been afraid of facing up to our identities?*

Could love have changed a lot of things and those changes looked so frightening and daunting?

Could be because love was bound to have changed us and the way we feel too?

We make a lot of noise.

We are human.

They have their failures just like we have ours too.

We couldn't really have done anything to make that much of a difference.

Years later we are to blame because we hadn't opened our eyes wide enough. One can't help but muse on what could have been unearthed had we opened our eyes wide enough. Maybe enough detractors to make us revise our decisions, maybe it could have been an eye-opener to the profound multifaceted complexities of a blindfold faith and identity. Maybe we could have stopped everything. But we didn't. We moved on and left a lot undone yet we still pretended we were satisfied with each other? These archaeologies of self are only re-reading the text of all that have been our vague pleasures with our love.

Their Wedding

"Looking after each other from today, in joys, in troubles, in riches, in rugs, in health, in illness...."

"Looking after our children in the way of Christ...."

"To shun away from behaviours that blacken our marriage..."

The "I do," the "I do." In a confident clear voice she says. He also says in a voice that really means it and at the end of the ceremony the Priest's words of wisdom as he says.

"Those united together in the name of the Lord should not allow their union to be broken by any living person. Now, I pronounce you husband and wife in the name of the Father, the Son and the Holy Spirit..."

And everyone in the congregation saying with aplomb. "Amen."

"You may kiss the bride."

"Wuhu," "umm," "uuh."

In a trance state everything happens to her as if there is a power or some force that is pushing her to say all that she has to say without any qualms or any dissuading thoughts. And it is time they move to the ceremony which is at their new home. They cut their cake and with laughter, tears and joy feed each other off their hands. There are a lot other celebrations. Some people asking them to kiss again, some for this and that so the day wears away and sooner it is evening and they are driven to the airport to catch an evening flight to their honeymooning destination in the magnificent island of Mauritius. They are now husband and wife. *Just like that!*

Their Marriage…, a train

They have become like a train, the drivers, or the passengers. They discover that the next stop where they were supposed to have stopped and got out of this train; it is too late for them to do that. There is acceptance of their fate standing on the front of their minds, blocking them from entering this platform. Sometimes it seems like the train has slowed down, in its tracks! Sometimes as if the train has abandoned them- the drivers! Sometimes as if they have abandoned the train- the passengers! Some other times as if the train's hypothetical announcement has died in their hearts. Sometimes it's like the twist of the past intertwining with the now, caught between then and now. All these details rule out a passion for life in the dull ashes of their marriage. Sometimes their marriage is like a dialogue, the dialogue between light and gold and in this fluttery of happiness of love they hope they would see to their marriage lasting in this very act of seeing to it that this train has reached its destination.

Their Lovemaking.., their infidelity.

Their lovemaking was always the awakening as of the sun yet it always left him drained and the more empty, making him the blanker, the more obsessed with Monalisa, thrusting him deeper and deeper into a much emptier world. It was always a lovemaking causing a death here and dreams over there, sometimes holding his love for his wife crumbling into chaos.

Foreplay

And so, into the heart-stopping tempos and climaxes again! He paws Monalisa's left girl; he cups her in his hands and she tells him she wants him to love her right girl the way he has loved her left girl so that he could stop her from feeling this wildly the way she is feeling about him. She tells him to suck her girls in his mouth so as to lick the wild fires of her hardened eyes. He takes hold of her right girl and as if he is about to swallow her in his mouth, he gulps the girl into his mouth. His tongue begins to make some circles around the eye as he licks her slowly and slowly. Like a child about to bite the mother's breast, he rakes the eye softly with his teeth. Monalisa's world is the world of pure sweet delicious pain and pleasure. She tells him she likes what he is still doing to her left girl whom his right hand is still cupping. His right hand is pushing her harder into her chest and when he does that she feels like she is about to crash down and faint with pleasure. She is a raging wildfire. She also knows that he can barely contain himself.

Her other mouth

She tells him she wants his mouth to find her other mouth. She slowly directs him downwards. He licks her neck, arms, fingertips, girls, eyes, again and again, the navel, thighs and vee... His mouth finds her crop and gets hold of that hotspot of her woman. He licks it. Her body is now fire itself. She tells him she wants to love him the way he has loved her. She seizes his molar into her hot and dry mouth. She starts licking its head and stroking it like as if licking a lollipop, like the sweet enchantress she was. His senses are consumed with pleasure, he can't contain himself anymore so he plunges his bristle cawing beak into the slickness of her soft women. They couple, like the overwhelming ravages of a bubonic plague. With hysterical intensity, they smear and immerse into a velleinage of pleasure. A flaming maelstrom of boiling rapids, canyons, precipitous currents, plunges or any kind of movement unawaiting or unafraid of any constraints that might reverse it, or divert it, refuse it, or refuse itself.

His thrusts.., her trusting…

He thrusts deeper and deeper into her, pumping harder and harder. The under-thrust reflective formations, swarms of ostracodes, condodorts, rhizodonts. She bellows, she shrieks, she caws like an erupting volcano. She opens deeper, pulling him in, deeper and deeper, wanting more, demanding... Wanting and wanting. Wanting…, until she couldn't help it any longer but cry out. *"Love you! Love you! Love you!"* He batters, cleaves and drives through with renewed vigour onto the mouth of her womb. *"Now, now, now love."* The tight, tight, long slope: He is barefoot sparrow running across flames, harder and harder, breathlessly.... Then he loses his footage! The sluggish extrusion of viscous lava like toothpaste, pillow lava like molten candle wax, he is falling and falling, tumbling and tumbling, like raindrops. Spurting-hot raindrops, drop after drop of his manly raining into her inviting mother earth, watering the plants, quenching their thirst, and bestowing life to the meadowlands. The irregular laying of mudstones and cherts, as irregular as the slow ticking of grandfather's clock, rhythmic with climactic cyclicity, their love grows, flowers and consummates. He dies between her silken honeyed thighs paying homage to renewed vows, faith and worship. And when he was inside her he felt vaguely aware that it would be un-good to reconcile himself to all those tainting antagonisms, values and morals, conceptions and travelled conclusions of their lovemaking, of their infidelity. When he was inside her he touched the primordial depths of the foundation of her animal soul.

84

After reading Arja Salafranca's poem "Snake."

His wife is trying to figure things too, in fact she pictures her life as of a tapeworm. It is burrowing into her skin, she is seeing it with her own eyes, entering her through her legs. She also knows that there is nothing that she can do about it. Most of it is already inside her legs, so she allows it to enter whole, believing that it would never survive her inside environment, believing her inner environment will change this tapeworm for the best. Humans have this innate belief that they can change other human beings. Everyone wants to be part of a miracle. But afterwards she starts to feel its... *suck, suck, sucking the blood and juices of her legs! Think; just think of its suck, suck, sound and feeling. Sometimes it brings out mucus, sometimes clotted blood and sometimes smelly sickly waters. Think of it as if it has been in her body for years and years, sucking her dry. See her ballooning rather than thinning out. One day it stops this sucking. It becomes dormant in her legs, nestled in the warm insides of her legs. Waiting for another suck, suck time.*

It sucks big time!

Then some day out into the future she discovers that it hasn't really been dormant. That it was silently chewing her insides. That all that is now in her insides is just a hollow space. The library of her gut is an empty parking lot. It is a life coming to (maybe out of) itself!

85

Her Struggles

She also discovers that all that she had given her husband, all the three healthy kids, all the warm affectionate love despite their always poor lovemaking. Their lovemaking that had become the code that shifted, weighed and swayed with the mass of the dying minutes of their marriage. It was now a marriage that was in shadows like a marriage cast-about by the magician's magical wand (wound). All those years of trying and trying to make him happy, all the tears and fears, heart breaks and archings, pains and hurts they shared- all that had come to nothing with him. These thoughts in her mind are like birthing a still-born; struggle, pain and then dead weight, which is a lot of trouble in itself, coming out distorted and dead, like a stillborn. She also discovers that she still wanted him but that she doesn't know why she still wanted him. Why he was still on her mind like those hills that sings silent songs of heartfelt sorrow. But she also knows that everything now depended on the distance that she would create between them. That distance would be the number of songs of heartfelt sorrows she could sing along the way to creating it.

Calling herself away

That deeper sense of having been wronged resurfaced again with deathly vengeance. She knows she can't call herself away from harming herself with this love that she still had for her husband. The love that is splitting that terrible space of gut-wrenching absence in her! *It is an epithelial loss*, of Jenna Marvis. *One catches oneself gripping for the next skin.* Most of the times we are always half way home and all that we need is for us to be cautious, steadfast and stay in the moment. Not to try to grab too much at one time. The subtlety of spite is when we individuate everything to a wandering greed like what her husband had been doing and grab everything, even more than what we ever needed

What she had talked about?

She had talked of her early childhood years in Nyamaropa irrigation area; the killing of her parents by the liberation forces during the liberation war because someone had lied to the liberation forces that they were conniving and working against the liberation cause. She had talked of how her grandmother, old and frail, had taken her in until when she died when she was still in her early teens. She had talked of her life in Nyakomba, north of Nyamaropa with her uncle, her mother's only brother. She had told the court that just before she completed her secondary school education that her Uncle had perished in the fatted Regina Caeli bus disaster so that she had moved in with her mother's only sister in Mbare Township, in Harare. She had told the court of how she had always felt like sad old clothes which are always handed down from one person to another without being asked whether she liked it or not. She had talked of meeting him in a bus journey from her rural home. How their relationship had grown. How she had helped him from there onwards; giving him a shoulder to cry on, a hand to hold, a heart to confide in... She had told the court of how she had always tried to make him happy even during their dating days. How he had always shut her out of his life. She had talked of how things had started changing with a year of seeing each other when he started opening up. How later he had let her in, in his trials and tribulations.

Their life together

She had talked about the proposal after many years of solid dating; their honeymooning, its beautiful sugar intensity and satisfaction. What it really meant to her. With grinding teeth she had talked about his dissatisfaction with their sexual relationship. How much she had bleed terribly emotional in trying to make him happy so that he couldn't leave their connubial nest. She had talked about hours upon hours spent engrossed in trying to understand how and when she had wronged him. The bad things she could have done. The harsh words she had exchanged with him; anything that could have been cause to this state of affair that was between them now. His drifting apart and endless nights upon nights spent all alone waiting for his return. She had talked about the infidelity, the fears, the tears, and the breath of the spiders' web she had explored, delved into and counted when the light was on. She had talked about the shadows when the light was out. Flitting, smearing and murmuring in inaudible voices, hauntingly hollow like her bowels. She had talked of the earliest silent hours of morning when sorrow came to its highest peak causing a sense of dislocation. Her love for him, becoming a tight prickly ball whirling deeper inside her breast's bottom, nettling like a nullifidian thorn. Hope sinking low into total misgivings and memory puffing up soft bellows of galling regret. Waiting and worrying up to the extent of dredging herself into quagmatic moods!

What she couldn't understand

She had talked of how she had started knitting in order to supplement her diminishing income. The hell that stretched from their sixth-year of marriage, how she had given birth to their third child in the streets on her way to the hospital. That she didn't have the monies to pay for ambulance fees. That when he came home with nothing, that she had paid for her hospital charges with her knitting monies. She had talked of what had made her almost kill Monalisa...

That she just couldn't understand why her husband had to sit inside the folded palm of the whirlwind preening his colourful feathers when she had all the August-mad filthy mercilessly slashed at her vulnerable frame.

All these things she told the people in the courtroom with bitterness everyone excused but not with an excuse for the deed she had done. That's how it happened and everyone accepted it as the truth...

Ploughing/ Accident/Hurricane...

We are ploughing in our fields at home. I am alternating people I am ploughing with. I see my brother; I am cultivating the field with him. It is the second field in our Musinga farm plot. But it feels like I am doing that for charity. They are names of huge UK celebrities I am ploughing out of the soil, and once I unearth them they have to pay off money in envelops towards charity. I see Prince Charles when he was young, a very athletic Charles. He stands there like he was the air, and somebody genuflects at him...

Later, I am the one to present the queen mother with her envelop. I feel so honoured.

*****

I am on way to the shops. I feel like I am with someone until I get to the base of the shops, at Doctor Dambasa's surgery building, it's a one floor high-rise, at the comer as you enter the shops. They are policemen directing traffic. I am told to walk on the near side of the street...

I follow the instruction. The atmosphere around the place suggests there has been an accident, hot wind itches through my clothing. At one time I want to just ignore it and move on to the shops where I am supposed to buy some things, but I turn my head, then I see the policeman holding the middle part of a person in his bare hands. It is dripping blood, and without the insides which seem to have been removed…and then my attention is attracted to the place where the policemen was coming from with that piece… I go there. It is so dark, I feel like a ghost. I look again. It has people surrounding it.

There are hands, legs, heads, ears…, and pieces of a person. My mind tells me to take a photo of it, but I say to myself it would be something I wouldn't know how to keep in the future. I don't take the photo. I feel crazed as the wind which whistles just to be sure of itself. I leave the scene.

*****

I have a programme I am running at some place…

*****

There is a certain guy who is trying to run an educational resources charity event to source stuff for the kids at the church. He has asked that people donate books, pencils, pens, writing pads etc. I ask him if literary journals can be counted under books. He thinks about it, and says 'no', he doesn't want them. I tell him it's his loss, for I have a lot of these and they could have helped these kids looking for learning resources. Are journals books?

*****

I am at the place of the family of two lovely girls. I am with the younger girl outside. At one time I am brushing my teeth and I throw up the Colgate toothpaste I was using on a tree at their gate. It looks like blood; I feel it in my nose. I am throwing out blood.

*****

We are talking with this younger sister when the mother comes out of the house. She is not friendly to me as she usually is. I am concerned but I know we will talk that out when she is ready. I enter their place. The older sister is inside, and the mother comes in. She tells me she is angry because I brought over my pots and pans and dumped them on her vestibule, rather than bringing them inside. I tell her it's not me who brought them over. It's the younger sister who wanted to clean them for me. It's her who has dumped them outside. We reconcile, she goes to sleep. I am with the older girl.

We are talking silently so that nobody would hear us, *intimately*. She tells me that she is not sleeping until way after midnight. She wants my company. We hang.., we get outside. The far eastern sky is raining hard. In my mind there is a hurricane of some sort out there, and my mind tells me there is going to eventually be a problem with the wind and water this side. I am talking to her about leaving the place. She wants to, but she needs her mother's permission. We are waiting for her to wake up. At one time she wakes up. I see her outside their property. She is walking around a heart ring of some beautiful marks in the road's soils and that heart looks (feels) like mine. She looks like a blowback where my loose heart will eternally fire.

Then the older girl is walking off, going the other direction...

Karidza

"Who is it?"

"Open the door!"

"Who is it, what do you want?"

"I said open the fucking door, Karidza!"

"It's the middle of the night, can't you see we are already asleep. Why don't you come early in the morning?"

"Hey Karidza, you heard what I said. Open the door or else..., just know that you will regret it." He knew what they meant. He knew he would be burned inside the house if he continues refusing them this.

Who could these people be? What did they want in the middle of the night? Did this have something to do with what's been going on throughout the whole country? He could only do as he had been told to do. He pushed the blankets to his feet, aimlessly rose from the bed, and so did his wife, Mai Karidza. He whispered to her softly that he wanted her to stay inside. She said she is not leaving him alone to face what was outside, that they were going to come inside the house anyway, to check there was no one inside. He tried to plead with her as she put on her night gown, but she now refused to even look at him, afraid he might dissuade her. She avoided his gaze as she accompanied him to the door. She knew she could only frighten him if he were to see the fear deep down her eyes.

They walked slowly to the door, unsure, like two young people who have suddenly aged, wondering why the problems always beset them, even when they thought they had done enough in a way to solving them or just coming to terms with. They were now old

94

people, Mai Karidza was in her late fifties, and Karidza himself was in his middle sixties. The two had failed to conceive a single child in their thirty-plus years of marriage. They had visited every faith healer they could think of and hear of; every Sangoma, everything, but failed. All that, it seemed now, had helped them to get closer to each other. They became closer and closer the more they failed, and now, they existed for each other, and for this dream they had for the country.

They were grassroots activist for DALP (Democratic Alliance Labour Party). They had been in a lot of hair rising situations before, fighting for this party, for their beliefs, for the other people's beliefs... They had survived beatings, injuries, attempted killings as they did their jobs. The logs kept falling in their paths, forcing them to keep jumping, even when they could barely walk. It was two years since they joined this party, in early 2001. Things were now haywire throughout the country.

At the door, Karidza heaved a heavy sigh as he prepared to open the door. He started opening the door slowly, trying to figure out what awaited him, but he was taken by surprise when a heavy boot smashed heavily on his left jaw from that left side, draining the oxygen gaspingly out of his lungs as he thudded to the floors like a bag of maize grains. His head was outside and the rest of his body was still inside piled on top of his wife, as Mai Karidza cried out in alarm and fear for her husband. She was also trying to raise herself from her husband.

The lights blinkered dangerously from an opening sky. It was a clear sky he was seeing even though it was, in actual fact, a dark night. The stars were coming down in a fast, fierce, transcendental traditional beat of the Jiti music hitting on the climax. They were

95

swirling, round around, like the swirl and dazzling acrobat drifts of the monkeys on tree's branches. But, before the stars could touch him, he gave in to the absorbing darkness which ensnared him soothingly.

Then, still deeper into this darkness, he felt the crack in his side body, and jolted back into consciousness as another boot slammed into his side, that hurt like he has never hurt before. He hallowed with pain, complementing his wife, who had been crying at a high voice as she begged them to stop beating her husband. Nobody seemed to hear their cries; nobody came to help them. They knew the next neighbourhood were hearing their cries but they also knew nobody was coming for the people of the next household were of this party. They knew they could only cry…or hope God would get into the minds of these thugs and stay them away from a killing orgy, but they also knew it was a futile hope.

And then he felt another kick slamming into his stomach, as another boot whammed his face as if kicking an inflated ball. The teeth came down from his gums like blooded gemstones as he grabbed his mouth trying to keep them inside his mouth but he knew he couldn't. He needed to release the pain inside his mouth, so he puked the teeth in a ball of blood, teeth, mucus and spit as another boot knocked the air out of his lungs by his chest, devastating him with pain as he fainted again.

He stared drifting from conscious to out of consciousness as they continued beating him. For long minutes he drifted in and out of consciousness as he still felt the cries of his wife, now being beaten as well, as she hallowed with the pain he now knew she was feeling all over her body. As one group continued beating him he knew the other group was beating his wife, as well. He knew there was nothing he could do about it, neither his wife. He came to the realisation that he had reached his endpoint in life. He was dying, but he had no regrets. He had faced the reality of his existence. He had tried all the best to achieve on the things he believed in. He knew the struggle would continue. It wouldn't end with their killings. As he folded for the last time he knew he was happy.

Printed in the United States
By Bookmasters